MICROHABITATS

Life in a
ROCK
POOL

Clare Oliver

Evans

Evans Brothers Limited

First published in Great Britain in 2002 by Evans Brothers Limited
2A Portman Mansions
Chiltern Street
London W1U 6NR

Project Editors: Sean Dolan, Tamsin Osler, Louise John
Consultant: Michael Chinnery
Production Director: Richard Johnson
Illustrated by Stuart Lafford
Designed by Ian Winton

Planned and produced by Discovery Books

British Library Cataloguing in Publication Data
Oliver, Clare
    Life in a rock pool - (Microhabitats)
    1. Tide pool animals - Juvenile literature
    I. Title
    578.7'699

    ISBN 0 237 52299 3

Printed in the United States

Contents

At the Shoreline

The Rock Pool

Rock pools, also called tidal pools, are found at the seashore, which is where the ocean or sea meets the land. Rock pools are made when crashing waves open up cracks or wear away hollows in the seashore rocks. No two rock pools are alike. The pools higher up the shore contain different life to those lower down because they are uncovered for longer.

gull

sea urchin

sea anemone

scallop

A Changing Habitat

Twice a day, when the tide comes in, rock pools are flooded by salty seawater. In summer, the hot sun can dry up the pools completely. In rainy weather, the pools fill with rain and the water becomes less salty. The animals and plants that live in rock pools have to be tough because their environment is always changing.

Guess What?

Rocks are a symbol of strength and solidity.

In China, crabs symbolise dishonesty because they move sideways rather than forwards.

The crab is the symbol for Cancer, one of the signs of the Zodiac.

limpet

crab

goby

starfish

dog whelk

shrimp

High and Low Tides

On most seashores, the **tide** rises and falls twice a day. At high tide, pools high up on the beach are filled with seawater.

At low tide, the sea goes out, leaving low-level pools that are normally underwater.

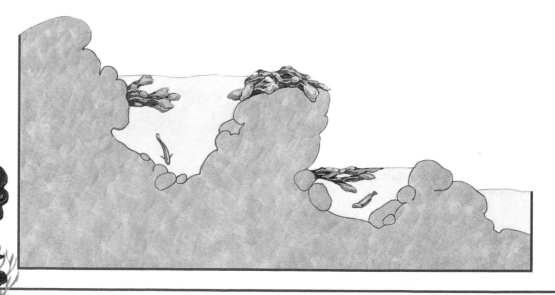

Gravity

Tides are caused by the **gravity** between the Moon and the Earth. As the Moon spins round the Earth, the pull of the Moon on the Earth makes the Earth's waters move.

The water on the part of the earth that is facing the Moon is pulled towards the Moon and the water level rises. This is a high tide. Because of this, the water level on the part of the earth furthest away from the Moon falls. This is a low tide. The Sun's gravity can affect the tides, too.

Exploring a rock pool can be fun, but it is important not to disturb the life in it.

Guess What?

At low tide, the sea goes out as far as 3km.

The fastest-moving tides occur in the Bay of Fundy, Canada. At high tide, the water can reach 21m above sea level.

Neap tides are not very high. They happen twice every month when the Sun and Moon pull in different directions.

Low Tide

The animals and plants that live in a rock pool have to adapt to the changes caused by the changing tides. At low tide, they are more exposed to the Sun or to the cold of the night – and to land-based **predators**! To protect themselves, soft-bodied shellfish close their shells, or burrow down into the sandy bottom of the pool.

Constantly changing conditions brought about by the tides make the tide pool a unique habitat.

High Tide

High tide can bring new difficulties for life in the pool. Shellfish attach themselves firmly to the rocks to protect themselves from the battering waves. High tide is feeding time, too, as the tide brings fresh **plankton** (microscopic plants and creatures) in from the sea. Barnacles extend their feathery legs and anemones wave their tentacles to pick up a meal.

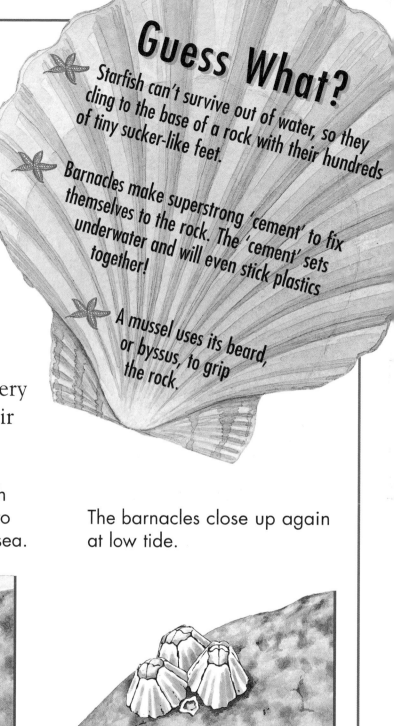

Guess What?

Starfish can't survive out of water, so they cling to the base of a rock with their hundreds of tiny sucker-like feet.

Barnacles make superstrong 'cement' to fix themselves to the rock. The 'cement' sets underwater and will even stick plastics together!

A mussel uses its beard, or byssus, to grip the rock.

Barnacles open their plates at high tide. They poke out feathery legs to pick up plankton swept in by the sea.

The barnacles close up again at low tide.

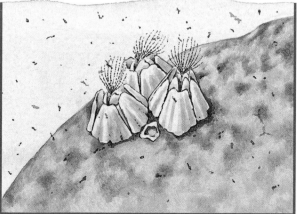

Rock Pool Plants

Seaweeds

Rock pools at the foot of the beach are nearly always covered by water. Slimy brown seaweed called kelp grows here, where it will not dry out. Higher up the beach, rock pools contain smaller seaweeds. Instead of having roots, seaweed clings to the rock with a tough stem called a holdfast.

Seaweeds are not really plants. They belong to a group of organisms called **algae** and can take in nutrients from the water through every part of their surface. There are green, brown and red seaweeds.

A Place to Hide

Seaweeds provide protection from the Sun and the wind for small creatures such as fish, crabs and molluscs. Hiding amongst the fronds is a good way to avoid being gobbled up by a gull, too! Seaweeds help animals in other ways – by producing oxygen for them to breathe, or as the source of a tasty meal.

Bladder wrack

Sea lettuce

Coral weed

Irish moss

See For Yourself

This kelp has scars where it's been nibbled by rock pool creatures.

The pouches on this piece of bladder wrack are filled with air, so the seaweed floats on the surface of the water.

11

Shellfish and Anemones

Clinging On

Many rock pool creatures have shells to protect them from predators.

Common periwinkle

Common limpet

Most shellfish belong to the group of animals called **molluscs**. Inside their hard shells they have soft, squishy bodies.

The ones that have shells with two halves, like mussels, cockles, scallops and oysters are called bivalves.

Variegated scallop

Mussel

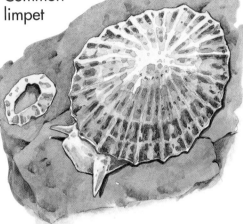

Molluscs with a single-piece shell are called gastropods. They include snails, whelks, limpets and periwinkles. Dog whelks are predators, but most gastropods graze on seaweed and other algae. Bivalves sift microscopic food from the water.

Periwinkles have hard, rounded shells to protect them from predators and the heat of the Sun.

See For Yourself

The colour of a dog whelk's shell says a lot about its diet. Yellow dog whelks eat pale-coloured barnacles, while purple ones eat mussels.

This 'path' on the rock shows where limpets have been grazing on seaweeds and other algae.

Scary Stingers

Sea anemones are beautiful rock pool creatures that come in all the colours of the rainbow. They might look like plants but they are scary predators that feed on tiny fish, shrimps and marine worms.

The elegant, waving tentacles of the sea anenome are armed with a painful stings to ward off predators or to stun **prey**.

Anemones belong to the same family as the wobbly jellyfish that live out at sea. Like jellyfish, they have very simple bodies and lots of waving tentacles.

Dinner Time

When an anemone catches a small shrimp or worm, it pulls it towards its mouth, which is at the centre of the tentacles and stingers. The meal is digested in the anemone's small stomach.

In this picture you can see the anemone's mouth surrounded by tentacles.

Guess What?

* Sea anemones are named after flowers. Long ago, people mistook their waving tentacles for petals.

* A sea anemone can divide itself into two to make two new complete creatures, but some produce tiny copies of themselves that swim out of their mouths!

* When it pulls in its tentacles at low tide, the strawberry anemone looks just like a juicy strawberry.

Rock Pool Creatures

Tiny Creatures

Thousands of tiny creatures swish in and out of the rock pool with the rising and falling tides. This mixture of floating plants and animals is called plankton.

The plants are known as phytoplankton and include different types of algae. Zooplankton is the name for the microscopic animals, eggs and **larvae** found in the seawater.

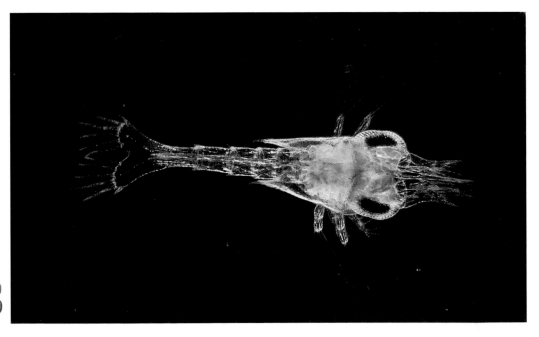

This lobster larvae was only 5mm long when it hatched!

Watery Nursery

Many of the young animals found in rock pools are the babies of shrimps, crabs and other **crustaceans** that breed in shallow waters. You might also find the eggs of various molluscs and fish. Some of these animals live in the rock pools until they are big and strong enough for life in the open sea. Others spend their whole lives in the rock pools.

This shrimp is carrying its eggs in an egg sack.

See For Yourself

This 'mermaid's purse' was a dogfish egg case. The baby fish developed in here for about 10 months before it hatched.

This pink string is the spawn of a sea hare, a seashore creature that looks a lot like a sea slug.

These egg cases are those of the common whelk. When they hatch, the whelks look exactly like miniature versions of their parents.

17

Starfish

There are lots of different types of starfish in rock pools. They range from cushion stars, which have plump bodies and five short rays (arms), to sunstars, which have lots of rays. Brittle stars have long, spindly rays.

At low tide, starfish hide under the rocks, but at high tide they come out to find mussels and other molluscs to eat.

Making a Meal of It

Starfish have a strange way of eating mussels! First, they wrench open a gap in the mussel's shell with their strong rays. Then they turn their own stomach inside-out, pushing it out of their mouth and into their victim's shell. When it has finished digesting the meal, the starfish swallows its own stomach again.

Guess What?

The starfish's eyes are on the end of its rays. Their eyesight is not like ours though, because they can only sense light and dark.

Not all starfish have five rays. Some have more than 50!

Starfish cling to the rocks with the hundreds of tiny suckers on their rays.

When a ray breaks off, the starfish can grow a new one

Common sunstar

Cushion star

Brittle star

19

Prickly Customers

The sea urchin's sharp spines provide good protection against its enemies – as you would quickly find out if you accidentally stepped on one! Their rounded bodies are covered with spines that, together with hundreds of suckered feet, help the animal to move around and even climb rocks.

The sea urchin's mouth is on the underside of its body. It has five strong teeth which it uses to scrape algae and tiny molluscs off the seaweed and rocks.

Sea urchins graze on algae, tiny molluscs, and seaweed, but they also eat the dead flesh of other animals when they can find it.

Strange Symmetry

Underneath the sea urchin's hundreds of spines and below its skin is a hard outer skeleton called a test. When a sea urchin dies, its spines break off and you can see the test in all its beauty. You might even have seen one washed up on the shore or in a shop at the seaside.

A sea urchin's test showing a section covered with spines and tube feet.

Suckered feet

Small holes where feet come out.

Spines

Raised bumps to which spines attach.

Guess What?

⭐ The beautiful shell-like tests of sea urchins are often sold as ornaments for the home.

⭐ The teeth and jaws of a sea urchin together are known as Aristotle's lantern, because the shape is like that of an old-fashioned lamp.

⭐ Humans are also predators of the sea urchin. Some consider the roe (eggs) to be a delicacy.

⭐ Some sea urchins can regrow their spines when they break off.

There are hundreds of bumps on a sea urchin's test. This is where the spines were attached. The rows of holes are where the tube-like legs came out from.

Crabs and Lobsters

As they scuttle between the rocks, crabs are the rock pool creatures that are perhaps the easiest to spot. They belong to the group of animals known as crustaceans. Lobsters and crayfish are crustaceans, too.

Crabs are shelled animals with five pairs of jointed legs and two pairs of antennae (feelers).

These animals scavenge for decaying bodies on the bottom of the rock pool.

Lobsters live for a very long time – sometimes until they are 80 to 90 years old!

Moving Home

When crabs and lobsters grow too big for their shells, they moult, shedding their old shell to reveal a shiny new one underneath. Hermit crabs are different. Only the front part of their body is covered with a shell – they look for old snail shells to protect their soft rear end.

Guess What?

Pea crabs are the tiniest crabs. You might even have found one on your dinner plate, because pea crabs live in the shells of mussels and oysters.

Green crabs aren't necessarily green! Males can be such a dark green they look black, while females and young come in all manner of patterns and colours.

Crustaceans can have up to 17 pairs of legs – some for walking and some for swimming.

Lobsters have blue blood!

As this hermit crab grows, it will need to find bigger snail shells to protect its body.

23

Smooth Swimmers

The rock pool habitat is too small, shallow and changeable to make a good home for most fish.

Rock pool fish like this blenny are usually quite small – between 5 and 20cm long.

Only small fish, such as blennies, gobies and sea scorpions live there all the time, feeding on small shrimps and other creatures. Sometimes, larger fish are swept in by the waves and get stranded in the rock pool between tides.

Special Features

Gobies, sea scorpions and blennies have adapted to life in the rock pool. Their eyes sit high on their head so they can check above for the shadow of a predator. Their mottled skins blend in with the rocks and pebbles, but they can also swim very fast. They dart into cracks in the rock if they sense danger.

Sea scorpions can turn lighter or darker for better **camouflage**.

Guess What?

Sea scorpions lay their bright orange eggs at the bottom of deep rock pools. The male guards the eggs until they hatch.

Blennies do not have scales, so their bodies are much smoother than other fish.

Sand gobies burrow into the sand to hide from predators.

Feathers and Fur

All sorts of other predators stop at the rock pool for a meal, especially hungry birds, such as gulls and oyster catchers. They pick through the seaweed and stones at low tide, looking for crabs, mussels and other food to eat. If a shell is too tough for a gull's strong beak to crack, it might drop it (from a great height) onto the rocks below, so that it smashes.

The rock pool is a good source of food for the strong-beaked gull.

Sea lions (found on the Pacific Coast of America) are close relations of the seals in Britain and also go to rocky shores to give birth to their pups.

Giving birth

The common seal and the grey seal are found around the coastline of Great Britain. They spend most of their lives at sea but gather together on the shores of rock pools to give birth to their pups, and to bask in the sunshine.

Rock Pools Under Threat

Changing Rock Pools

The force of the waves wearing on the rocks and sand constantly changes a rock pool, but this change takes place very slowly. **Global warming** – a rise in the Earth's temperature – could lead to higher sea levels in years to come, leaving today's rock pools under water. Other changes are caused by **pollution**, which changes the coastline and harms rock pool organisms.

Rubbish left behind by humans or washed in by the sea can destroy the balance of the rock pool microhabitat.

Polluted Pools

Estuaries are the place where rivers meet the sea. Some have become dumping places for dangerous chemicals from factories and farmland or for sewage from our homes. These poisons are absorbed by tiny plankton. Larger animals, such as mussels, then feed on the plankton. In this way pollutants travel right up the **food chain** into even bigger animals, including humans.

Oil spills are another problem – when huge tankers carrying crude oil leak or run aground, life along the shore suffers and some species can disappear forever.

Glossary

Algae: Plant-like organisms, such as seaweeds, that live mainly in water. Like plants, algae make energy from sunshine, but they are not plants because they do not have leaves stems or roots.

Camouflage: Colouring, or a means of disguise, that makes an animal blend in with its surroundings so that it is more difficult for predators to see.

Crustaceans: Armour-covered animals such as crabs. They have jointed legs, like insects. Most have at least five pairs. Crustaceans live in water.

Food chain: A series of plants and animals in a microhabitat that are linked because each becomes food for the next one in the series. Large predators seem to be at the top (or end) of the food chain, but when they die they rot down and feed new plants or algae which are nearer the bottom of the food chain.

Global warming: A rise in the world's temperatures, which may be caused by more greenhouse gases such as carbon dioxide in the air. These gases act like greenhouse glass to keep in the Sun's heat. Higher temperatures will make icebergs melt and sea levels rise.

Gravity: The force that pulls an object toward a heavier object. The gravity of the Moon pulls the waters of the oceans in different directions as it spins around the Earth.

Larva: An animal baby, such as a beetle grub, that looks nothing like its parent. Many crustaceans pass through one or more larval stages.

Microhabitat: A small, specialised place, such as a rock pool or freshwater pond, where particular animals live and plants grow.

Molluscs: Boneless animals with soft, squishy bodies that need to be kept damp and are sometimes protected by a shell. Snails, mussels and squid are all types of molluscs.

Plankton: A mix of plants and animals that drift on the surface of the sea. Many are so small they can only be seen through a microscope.

Pollution: Damage to the environment, caused by human actions. Sewage pumped into the sea is a type of water pollution. Exhaust fumes from cars are a type of air pollution.

Predators: Animals that hunt other animals for food.

Prey: Animals that are hunted by other animals for food.

Tides: The regular rise and fall of the sea.

Acknowlegdements

The publishers would like to thank the following for permission to reproduce their pictures:
Front cover: Richard Herrmann/Oxford Scientific Films; p.7: Greg Balfour Evans/Greg Evans International; p.8: David Woodfall/Natural History Photographic Agency; p.10: Charles & Sandra Hood/Bruce Coleman Collection; p.13: N.R.Coulton/Natural History Photographic Agency; p.14: Rodger Jackman/Oxford Scientific Films; p.15: Fritz Polking/Frank Lane Picture Agency; p.16: D.P.Wilson/Frank Lane Picture Agency; p.17: Kim Taylor/Bruce Coleman Collection; p.18: Richard Herrmann/Oxford Scientific Films; page 20: William S.Paton/Bruce Coleman Collection; p.22: Charles & Sandra Hood/Bruce Coleman Collection; p. 23: PhotoDisc inc.; p.24: Charles & Sandra Hood/Bruce Coleman Collection; p.25: Roy Waller/Natural History Photographic Agency; p.26: Jeff Foott/Bruce Coleman Collection; p.27: Tui de Roy/Oxford Scientific Films; p.28: Paul Kay/Oxford Scientific Films; p.29: E & D Hosking/Frank Lane Picture Agency.

Index